Community Care in Action: The Role of Costs

Proceedings of a conference
held on 17 May 1993

edited by
Jennifer Beecham and Ann Netten

© Crown Copyright 1993

No part of this publication may be reproduced in any form without the permission of the Department of Health

Typeset and published by the Personal Social Services Research Unit and printed by the University of Kent Printing Unit

PSSRU
University of Kent at Canterbury
Canterbury
Kent
CT2 7NF
England

ISBN 0 904938 40 9

PSSRU publications

PSSRU Studies: works of scholarship of long-run importance, published under the Ashgate imprint.

PSSRU Monographs: publications (typically short book length) for faster reporting of research and argument, published by the PSSRU itself.

Research & Policy Papers and *Discussion Papers.*

Bulletins: the PSSRU Bulletin (giving an overview of the Unit's activities) is available free on application and other Bulletins are produced reporting on individual programmes of work.

Contents

Acknowledgements iv

Contributors v

Costing community care: background to the book and the day
Jennifer Beecham and Ann Netten 1

The importance of cost information
Clive Smee 5

The dangers of inappropriate or poor quality information
Ken Wright 11

The roles of costs research
Martin Knapp 17

The problems presented in practice in local authorities
Mary Richardson 27

Common issues — costs in health and social services
Chris Gostick 37

Approaches to compiling and using cost information
David Claridge 45

Performance measurement and value for money
David Browning 53

Messages of the day
Jennifer Bernard 57

Acknowledgements

We wish to thank all those who helped make the conference of which this is the record such an enjoyable and, we hope, useful day. Our thanks are due to the speakers — David Browning, David Claridge, Chris Gostick, Martin Knapp, Mary Richardson, Clive Smee and Ken Wright — for their valuable contributions, and to Jennifer Bernard for her admirable chairing of the proceedings.

Our thanks are also due to those from the PSSRU who helped make the day run so smoothly, in particular to Anne Walker (whose organisational abilities never cease to amaze us) and Anita Whitley who assisted her. Many thanks too to Nick Brawn, who was responsible among other things for the conference pack, a poster session on the day and the presentation of this volume.

Jennifer Beecham
Ann Netten

Contributors

JENNIFER BEECHAM is a Research Fellow in the PSSRU, which she joined after graduating in social policy and administration from the University of Kent at Canterbury in 1986. She has seven years involvement in the economics of mental health care programme, evaluating services for a variety of client groups and collaborating with a number of other research teams. Other areas of research are the examination of child care assessment services and involvement in the unit costs working group. She is a former residential social worker.

JENNIFER BERNARD was at the time of the conference General Manager, Community Care, for Birmingham Social Services Department, and has since become Director of Newcastle Social Services. She joined Birmingham SSD in the Spring of 1992 from Kent Social Services. During her six years in Kent she held a variety of posts, including Assistant Director with responsibility for the introduction of the Children Act and the NHS and Community Care Act. She has worked in the private and voluntary sectors and is particularly interested in the delivery of care services as well as planning and theorising about them. She remains optimistic about the future of community care.

DAVID BROWNING is Associate Director for Health and Social Service Studies at the Audit Commission. He has worked on community care issues since joining the Audit Commission in 1985. Before that he worked at the Department of Health and Dorset Social Services Department.

DAVID CLARIDGE has worked in the social services field since 1979. His initial experience was in administration and finance and he was Assistant Director of Social Services with that brief for six years. For the last four years he has been the Assistant Director of Social Services responsible for adult services in the London Borough of Croydon. As lead officer responsible for implementing community care in the borough he oversaw the production of its first community care plan and the achievement of the 'eight key tasks' identified in the landmark first Foster/Laming letter. In September 1992, at the invitation of the Minister for Health, he became a core member of the Community Care Support Force, involving a secondment to the Department of Health almost full time to December 1992, and then as a part-time core member until the Support Force was disbanded at the beginning of April. His role in the Support Force included a particular interest in financial issues and latterly those relating to IT.

CHRIS GOSTICK was Director of Social Services for Westminster City Council until early 1993, and is now Community Care Development Manager for North West Thames Regional Health Authority. He has been Associate Lecturer and Visiting Research Fellow at the University of Surrey since 1980, with a particular interest in personal social services research, and is Secretary to the Association of Directors of Social Services (ADSS) Services Evaluation, Research and Information Committee.

MARTIN KNAPP is Professor of the Economics of Social Care and Deputy Director of the Personal Social Services Research Unit, University of Kent at Canterbury. He is the author of many books and articles which address or report evaluations of health and social care. His most recent books, both co-authored, are *Care in the Community: Challenge and Demonstration*, (Avebury 1992) and *Social Care in a Mixed Economy*, (Open University Press 1993). His current research focuses on the developing mixed economy of care; services for people with mental health problems; and the voluntary sector.

ANN NETTEN is a Research Fellow at the Personal Social Services Research Unit. She has a background of local authority social services research, particularly into services for elderly people. At the PSSRU she has been developing a theoretical framework for the social care of elderly people. Her other work has included costing informal care, services for elderly people and criminal justice services.

MARY RICHARDSON is Director of Social Services, London Borough of Waltham Forest, Joint Honorary Secretary of the London

Branch Association of Directors of Social Services, and Chair of the Greater London post qualifying education and training consortium.

CLIVE SMEE has been Chief Economic Adviser to the Department of Health since 1989. He has wide experience of a variety of government departments, acting as Economic Adviser to ODM, Central Policy Review Staff and HM Treasury. In the course of this he has developed a number of international links, acting as consultant to the New Zealand Treasury and Department of Health and chairing the OECD working party between 1987 and 1990.

KEN WRIGHT is Deputy Director of the Centre for Health Economics at the University of York. He has worked on health economics for the last twenty-one years. His research interests lie in the economics of health and social care of people with long-term disabilities. Before this, he worked in local government and as a lecturer in further education.

Costing community care: background to the book and the day

Jennifer Beecham and Ann Netten
Personal Social Services Research Unit

This volume draws together papers presented at a conference organised by the Personal Social Services Research Unit (PSSRU), University of Kent at Canterbury. The purpose of the conference was to bring together some of the many different perspectives on costs in the current care environment: Department of Health, researchers, the Audit Commission and in particular those at the sharp end: local and health authorities.

Clive Smee, Chief Economic Adviser to the Department of Health, opens the debate by describing the Department's concerns, priorities and activities in the field of costing community care. The research perspective is represented in the next two chapters. Ken Wright from CHE, University of York, discusses some of the pitfalls associated with inappropriate use of cost information. Martin Knapp, PSSRU, goes on to identify the value of cost research, drawing on a variety of completed and ongoing studies.

An important element of the research perspective is the relationship between research, policy and practice: research is borne from policy and practice argument, empirical research then feeds and develops these arguments which, in turn feed and develop the research arena. By definition, it is a symbiotic relationship and, also by definition, it is a long-run process. One example is the programme of experiments in care-management, research which the PSSRU began more than sixteen years ago and which has fed directly into local and national policy and practice.

However, the immediate impetus for organising the conference came from the publication of the book *Costsing Community Care: Theory and Practice* (Netten and Beecham, 1993), which was compiled in response to the increased level of interest in the field of costs. The PSSRU has a long history of estimating costs of services as knowledge of the resource implications of services or innovatory models of service delivery is central to the 'production of welfare' approach to evaluation. The book describes theoretical and pragmatic issues that need to be taken into consideration when estimating and using costs and describes four case studies based on work by members of the PSSRU.

A subsequent report, *Unit Costs of Community Care 1992/1993* (Netten and Smart, 1993), builds on this work and takes it forward by bringing together detailed cost information from a variety of sources. The report provides a building block design for calculating unit costs which allows users to construct service costs as their data become available. These building blocks are presented in service *schemata* which initiate a standardised approach to costing services, adaptable for a number of purposes. The report also provides 'state of the art' cost estimations for a variety of health and social care services. These are nationally applicable costs culled from a variety of sources: current research; professional associations; and publicly available data. Up-dated and extended reports from the research will be available at regular intervals. Furthermore, this project is just one element of an on-going programme of Department of Health funded work on unit costs.

Costs, of course, should carry a health warning, for they make people nervous. This response is often caused by lack of information: not knowing how costs can be calculated; not knowing how someone else's costs were calculated; not knowing what the data mean; not knowing what to do with the data; not knowing what others will make of the same data; and not knowing what everybody else is doing about costs.

These are, perhaps, the unfortunate consequences of the way costs are perceived. Costs and care, to quote one author in *Costing Community Care*, are still uncomfortable bedfellows. Furthermore, although one of the underlying objectives of the NHS and Community Care Act is clarification of the way resources are used, enabling better use of resources in the provision of care services, the new competitive care climate is tending to breed secrecy. The search for a level playing field has bought forth cries of 'but it places us at a disadvantage if our competitors know our costs'.

Such secrecy can foster misunderstandings which may well foster inefficiency. Costs issues are often approached in different ways but if the approach used in any one context is not made clear it is likely the resulting cost data will be viewed with some misgivings. The improved basis for decision-making at which we are all aiming then becomes suspect.

The first requirement to resolve this dilemma is *clarity* of information. Information, such as that contained in the two publications mentioned above, is founded on many peoples' research experience in facing and solving problems in costs. The information in these publications is not perfect but clearly explains the current status of costs research.

The second requirement is *exchange* of information. The research perspective, identified above, is just one of many. The perspective that will have the most direct impact on users of services is that of those involved in estimating and using cost information at the purchaser and provider level.

Three papers reflect this local perspective. Mary Richardson, Director of Waltham Forest Social Services, describes some of the problems facing local authorities currently involved in producing costs data. Chris Gostick, Community Care Manager, North West Thames Regional Health Authority, examines the issues raised by the need to integrate health and social services more effectively. David Claridge draws on both his experience with the Support Force and in Croydon Social Services Department to describe approaches to resolving some of the difficulties identified.

The Audit Commission has established itself as a key influence on local authorities. David Browning describes the current activities and concerns of the Audit Commission in the area of costing social services. In the last chapter, Jenny Bernard (Birmingham Social Services), who chaired the conference, draws together the main messages from the day.

In bringing together these different perspectives the conference, and this volume, are steps in the direction of information exchange, encouraging the interdependence of research, policy and practice identified above. The information exchanged should form the basis for future work to make cost information both accurate *and* useful.

REFERENCES

Netten, A. and Beecham, J. (eds) (1993) *Costing Community Care: Theory and Practice*, Ashgate, Aldershot.

Netten, A. and Smart, S. (1993) *Unit Costs of Community Care 1992/93*, PSSRU, Canterbury.

The importance of cost information

Clive Smee
Chief Economic Adviser, Department of Health

INTRODUCTION

I would like to focus here on the timeliness of this conference, to emphasise the reasons why the Department of Health attaches great importance to costs and costs analysis, and to outline the Department's current support for improving the quality of cost information. I will end with some comments on the directions in which costs research might go next.

TIMELINESS

It is now seven weeks since the full implementation of the community care reforms and social service departments have new responsibilities and substantial new monies. Their tasks, with an emphasis on the purchaser/provider split, developing the mixed economy of care, care management and the potential development of devolved budgets, all increase the importance of valid and reliable cost information. At one level the reforms are about clarification of the ways in which resources are used. In economists's terms, the reforms are also about introducing transparency into relationships. Efficient markets, economists generally agree, require accurate and accessible information. Secrecy could undermine the reforms and the Department is likely to look unfavourably on secrecy within the social services environment, just as within the developing internal market in health care.

THE IMPORTANCE OF COSTS INFORMATION

Costs information should not just benefit the Department, local authorities or economists. The critical question, as Mary Richardson will remind us, is how will clients benefit from better cost information? I suggest they can, and should, benefit in five ways.

First, from overall budgets that are of more appropriate size. Information on costs can support arguments about the total size of budgets, including the annual discussions between the Department and the Treasury within the public expenditure round. Second, clients will benefit from the promotion of more equitable treatment; better costs data can assist in the equitable allocation of resources, for example, in the improvement of the formula for the Standard Spending Assessments. Third and fourth, clients will also benefit from the development of more effective policies and from the early termination or re-focusing of ineffective policies. Cost-effectiveness analysis is widely accepted as essential to ensure the most effective deployment of resources and as a critical element in the ex-post evaluation of policies. Fifth, costs information creates pressures for a more efficient use of resources to benefit clients. Good cost information can generate comparisons ('yardstick competition') and assist with efficient pricing. All this should help to ensure that a limited amount of resources delivers the maximum care services.

All organisational levels involved in community care need good cost information if they are to achieve the objective of maximising delivery of care within existing resources. This is as true of the Department as it is of local authorities; as true of commissioners as it is of providers; and as true of the public sector providers and voluntary agencies as it is of private sector providers. For example, for the last two years, the Department was able to use PSSRU costs data to argue with the Treasury about the introduction of assessments and how much they would cost. Without that data we almost certainly would have received fewer resources. One important example of the need for good costs data in local authorities are the new criteria for eligibility for payments from the Independent Living Fund. The ILF cannot make payments to clients unless the social services department agrees to provide a package of non-residential care costing at least £210 per week, gross of charges to the client. Authorities will need to have information on the costs of the domiciliary services they provide or purchase in order to show that they have clients of such dependency.

So the requirement for better costs information is not a theoretical one, it is real. Costs data could impact in a real way on the services which clients receive through local authorities.

SUPPORT FOR IMPROVING COSTS INFORMATION

In addition to attending this conference in some force the Department is supporting a programme of research to encourage and facilitate the production and use of good quality costs data.

The Department funded the work represented in *Costing Community Care: Theory and Practice* (Netten and Beecham, 1993) and *Unit Costs of Community Care 1992/1993* (Netten and Smart, 1993) as well as other valuable costing work at York. Indeed wherever possible the Department insists that community care research should include a costing element. For example, cost-effectiveness analysis will be at the heart of research-based evaluations of the community care reforms. We are currently funding work to discover the reasons for higher unit costs of personal social services in Inner London and to distinguish avoidable and unavoidable factors (see chapter 6 of *Costing Community Care*). This work is expected to inform the current review of the Standard Assessment formulae.

The Department also recognises the importance of improving knowledge of local unit costs. As Bleddyn Davies has said in the Epilogue of *Costing Community Care*:

> ... the national averages of relative prices of service options are just that: national averages concealing big variations. These averages would grossly distort equity and efficiency in individual areas if applied as policy criteria locally.

In recognition of this fact, our statistics division is leading the work on unit costs under the Department's *Personal Social Services Information Strategy*. This Strategy is the 'umbrella' within which the Department is considering what changes need to be made to statistical returns for personal social services (PSS) activity, staffing and finance data in the light of the recent legislation. The aim of this review is to ensure a consistent approach is made to identifying the data needed and the gaps and overlaps which need to be avoided. Within this strategy, the Unit Costs Project is being taken forward in phases. The first phase is to recommend changes which could be made in the short term and two areas are currently under consideration: the definitions of services and service costs for various activities, staffing and expenditure returns with a view to ensuring data complementarity, and the treatment of capital costs and re-charging of overheads to specific services and client groups. Following an initial report by the PSSRU (Bebbington et al., 1992), the management consultants KPMG conducted a study involving discussions with a number of local authorities (KPMG Peat Marwick, 1993). The Department is likely to propose both short and long term improvements to existing data collections and will, of course, consult local authority associations about these.

THE FUTURE

The Department's priorities for pure costing work are already reflected in, and were perhaps borne from, the thinking of the PSSRU (see, for example, the editorial of *Unit Costs of Community Care 1992/1993*). These priorities include the development of cost information about services for children and families; the development of approaches to the estimation of the costs of day services, resource centres and other innovative services; the development of approaches to professional time use; and finally, the improvement of capital and overhead estimates. These priorities link naturally with the Department's wider research priorities and with our policy and service development priorities in community care. The interactions within the programme can be quite complex. For example, the PSSRU intends to conduct a further study to look at targeting, costs, outcomes and cost-effectiveness of social care for elderly people. This will provide comparison data for the findings from the 1985 study on the same subject. (Davies, Bebbington, Charnley and colleagues, 1990). Fieldwork from this follow-up study and from other work at the PSSRU and the Centre for Health Economics at York will provide data for the Unit Costs Programme which in turn will provide methodological approaches to assist these broader pieces of research.

Costs data also needs to be complemented with agreed outcome measures, and the Department is funding a range of work on various aspects of outcome measurement. This is an area often raised in the Department, particularly during the public expenditure rounds. How do we judge the success of community care? How do we judge whether we are making effective progress? What should be our criteria for measuring the outcomes of community care? There are currently a large number of possible answers to these questions but few that are widely accepted. The development of *agreed* outcome measures is the obvious complement to improved work on costs. We would welcome a conference, similar to this one, on this issue in two or three years.

In the meantime I look to this conference to provide further guidance on future research priorities in the area of costs and cost analysis.

REFERENCES

Bebbington, A. C., Kelly, A., Netten, A. and Schneider, J. (1992) Unit cost estimation for Personal Social Services: Step 1 Report, PSSRU Discussion Paper 899/2.

Davies, B., Bebbington, A. C., Charnley, H. and colleagues (1990) *Resources, Needs and Outcomes in Community-Based Care,* Ashgate, Aldershot.

KPMG Peat Marwick (1993) Unit Costs of Personal Social Services, KPMG, London.

Netten, A. and Beecham, J. (eds) (1993) *Costing Community Care: Theory and Practice,* Ashgate, Aldershot.

Netten, A. and Smart, S. (1993) *Unit Costs of Community Care 1992/93,* PSSRU, Canterbury.

The dangers of inappropriate or poor quality information

Ken Wright
Centre for Health Economics, University of York

INTRODUCTION

Costing studies are frequently controversial. In part, this is because all the information needed to produce accurate results is rarely available and short-cuts have to be taken, assumptions have to be made about missing data and approximate values have to be employed to ensure studies meet tight deadlines. Consequently, there are continual arguments about the methods used to build up cost estimates, about alternative sources of data and about using different assumptions. The main aim of this paper is to remind ourselves of the different purposes and contexts of costing studies and the need to be clear about information sources, their use and the attempts to make the best of less than perfect data.

CHARACTERISTICS OF COST INFORMATION

Costs are *specific to decisions and contexts*. Typical uses for costs data include:

- Charging policies;
- Evaluation of service innovations and development;
- Comparisons of performance or audit within or across agencies.

It is therefore very important to ensure that costs developed for one purpose are not transposed to another without careful consideration of the different methods which are relevant to one use and not another. For example, full cost charging of overheads might be important for pricing decisions but not for service evaluation, because of the different scales of operations which are relevant to the two uses. Cost comparisons within and across agencies also have to proceed with caution to ensure that all the items included in one activity are included in the other. For example, in comparing costs of providing residential care for elderly people across authorities, the accounting conventions differ and it is necessary to standardise all the accounts before any comparison can be made.

One of the most important contexts of costing exercises is whether we are concerned with resource use or cash flow: that is the *economic* or the *financial* concepts of costs. The present financial climate with its emphasis on the welfare of taxpayers and its use of cash-limited budgets tends to focus our attention on cash flows into and out of individual agencies (the financial aspect of costs). If, however, we are concerned about resource use as a whole, the economic concept of opportunity cost is the appropriate basis, and this has two implications. First, that we need to question whether the cash paid for a resource reflects its opportunity cost (the value of that resource in its alternative use) and second, that all resources used are costed irrespective of the organisation or individual who 'owns' them. It is very easy to miss some aspects of resource use. For example, residential care costs often miss the input of services (e.g. paramedical or day services) used by some residents and comparisons across homes may not be valid if some homes have been allocated these costs and others have not.

This is not to assert that one basis is superior to another, rather that if one basis is chosen it should be uniformly applied and its limitations acknowledged. For example, using economic costs may ignore the political importance of spending by particular agencies while financial costs can indicate that one agency is staying within its budgetary constraints but may fail to show how costs are passed on to other organisations or individuals.

Costs are *specific to time, location and output*. Some services or projects involve different time profiles of expenditure, normally those that involve heavy capital expenditure at some stage in their development. Since expenditure made immediately is pound for pound more valuable than expenditure made sometime in the future, the timing of cash flows needs to be carefully identified and the appropriate rate of discount needs to be applied to reflect these different values. It is also important that cost profiles are monitored over time to check how resource use or expenditure changes. For example, schemes or policies may seem very expensive if they need special staff training at their outset, but may become cheaper than the current alternative as staff adjust to the new work.

Relative price changes are also important when considering the evaluation of alternative ways of achieving an objective. Schemes which use different mixes of inputs may alter in relative value if the price of one input changes differently from another. For example, residential and day services have recently had to take account of changing values of land and property. These problems are not so much affected by poor information as by general uncertainty and difficulties in forecasting price changes.

Costs *vary by location* for a number of reasons. First, input prices are higher in some localities, and second, delivery of peripatetic services (for example, community nursing) may be more difficult in some areas because of population scatter or traffic congestion. Third, some services have different input mixes for historical reasons. These variations warn against comparing or transferring costs across localities without making the necessary adjustments. This does not mean we do not have to take short cuts at times. There is often a lack of specific information on the services, so we use 'borrowed' information. For example, day services are often difficult to cost and one relies on work done in another locality. This is usually acceptable, provided that the facilities have a similar profile, but local variations in the type or scale of provision should make us wary of using this procedure.

Costs are *sensitive to output* and the relationship between output and capacity constraints. Costing methodology is closely related to the methodology of outcome measurement. Many of our unit costs for services use very routine output measures, for example hours of help provided, cases, visits, resident or patient days. The implicit assumption behind these measures is that they are homogeneous units of output. We know this is not true in terms of both the characteristics of service users and the quality of service delivered. Thus, we can be in danger of making false comparisons of costs or estimating service development costs incorrectly if we do not allow for these variations. The classic distinction between average and marginal costs is very relevant to the need for clarity on present and future levels of output and capacity constraints. This is where the different uses of cost information is so important. Marginal costs are frequently needed for evaluative exercises which are concerned with changes in the scale of operations of different services, for example, more care at home and less provided at day centres. Average costs are important for pricing decisions and to ensure that all costs are covered. It is, therefore, very important that cost information is set within its decision framework and assumptions about the future scale of operations are clearly stated.

CONCLUSION

Costing work is rarely straightforward. It frequently demands making the best use of the information available rather than having all the information needed. This pushes us into making assumptions such as the allocation of managerial overhead costs between different services in proportion to the total spend or perhaps assuming that fieldwork staff spend a certain proportion of their time travelling. The use of one rate of discount is also subject to certain assumptions about social time preferences.

There are two major implications of this lack of certainty in our work. First, we have to subject our assumptions to sensitivity analysis. How do different methods of allocating overheads work? What would be the effect of applying different rates of interest? Although sensitivity analysis clutters up the work and produces a range of costs rather than a single point estimate, it is important to clarify and test our assumptions.

Second, cost calculations have to be made available for public scrutiny. We have to express our doubts, expose our uncertainties, identify our information sources and qualify our data in an open manner so that others may question what we have produced. A considerable amount of openness is created through audit of services and, in research, through peer review of scientific papers. It is to be hoped that the new competitive world of health and community care will increase the transparency of all costing work.

The roles of costs research

Martin Knapp
Deputy Director, Personal Social Services Research Unit

INTRODUCTION

If the next book from the PSSRU were to be titled *The Recent History of the Demand for Costs* there could well be five chapters. Each chapter could describe a period in which a particular attitude to costs research dominated. The first chapter, 'Benign Neglect' would refer to a period before the world-wide economic depression of the 1970s, and would describe social and health care decision-making before costs became a major issue. Costs research was certainly undertaken but the demand for costs information, other than that provided by finance departments, was low.

'Wilful Castigation' would be the title of the second chapter, describing how economists were seen as Hannibal Lecters of the late 1970s. Costs research and the resulting data were seen as linked to the downward trend in public spending. Some people even seemed to subscribe to the view that costs research could *cause* public expenditure cuts. To describe the early 1980s there would be a chapter on the 'Hurried Reorientation' of attitudes to costs. The importance of costs research was recognised during these years but the chapter is short, almost an introduction to chapter 4: 'Smash and Grab'. The distinguishing activity in this phase is the dangerously unselective grasping of whatever costs data are available, no matter how poorly defined or measured.

The outlook for the 1990s is certainly more encouraging. It would be described in a chapter on 'Construction and Illumination' which would examine the discerning and purposive planning of costs research and its utilisation to aid policy and practice.

BACKGROUND

This paper focuses on the contents of this (putative) chapter 5. I want to examine what costs research has to offer policy, planning and practice. Research is an activity which, for at least part of the time, is slightly remote from the policy and practice processes. It can be more reflective than the routine, day-to-day handling of costs and other evidence by those agencies which plan and deliver community care. The research perspective has the advantage of taking a broader view where the wood can hopefully be seen for the trees. In principle, it can more easily tackle longer term issues.

The context is set by the demands of the real world and the conceptual framework in which research is interpreted. To describe the real world context I will use a simple representation of the mixed economy of social care and the many transaction types within it. Diagram 1 gives some examples of social care services and the different provider types and means of purchase or funding that may be associated with them (Wistow, Knapp, Hardy and Allen, 1994). Local authority field social work services, for example, are provided within and funded by the public sector. These services are funded through *coerced collective demand*, that is, the public sector purchases the services on behalf of citizens, and services are funded through tax revenues. By contrast, an example of *uncoerced collective demand* would be voluntary organisations funded by donations. Parental payments for voluntary sector pre-school day care are an example of *uncompensated individual consumption*, where there is no subsidy from social security payments (as there may be for board and lodging payments).

The real world of the mixed economy is more complex than this summary diagram but even so, *inter alia*, we can see that the mixed economy is already well developed and we know that we can expect further evolution over the 1990s. More important for today, there are

Diagram 1
The mixed economy matrix: social care examples

PURCHASE, DEMAND OR FUNDING	PROVISION OR SUPPLY OF SERVICES			
	Public sector	Voluntary sector	Private sector	Informal sector
Coerced collective demand	Local authority field social work services	Contracted-out day care	Publicly-funded placements in private residential homes	Foster family care for children funded by SSD
Uncoerced or voluntary collective demand	Voluntary organization payments for public sector training programmes	Self-help group paying for expert advice from larger voluntary organisation	Purchases of goods and services by Mind or Age Concern	Foster family placements arranged and funded by Barnardo's
Corporate demand	Private residential home payments for LA registration and inspection	Corporate donations to charities	Private nursing home purchases of food, electricity, etc.	Employers' payments for employees' childminding
Uncompensated individual consumption	User charges for LA home help support	Parental payments for pre-school day care	Payment for private residential care by family or resident	Private childminder services
Compensated individual consumption	LA residential home fees backed up by pensions	Board and lodging payments to voluntary homes	Housing benefit and other user subsidies for private housing	Purchases from community care grants
Individual donation (for use by others)	Volunteers working in LA intermediate treatment unit	Donations to the Children's Society or Mencap	Volunteers in private residential homes	Intra-family transfers of resources and care

a host of transaction types and policy issues which require a research agenda to address numerous pressing questions. The simplest would be to ask what are the outcomes and costs of care in a mixed economy?

Obviously, research needs to be based in the real world, but it also needs to be based on a sound conceptual framework. Ronald Reagan might have been slightly unkind when, in one of his speeches, he defined an economist as someone who sees something working in practice and then wonders if it will work in theory. Nevertheless, he was right to identify the economist's concern that empirical research should not be conducted in a conceptual vacuum.

In the PSSRU's eighteen-year history the conceptual framework that has had a major influence is the *production of welfare*. This approach distinguishes outcomes from inputs and costs, and stresses the need for the careful examination of links between them. The basic assumption is that final and intermediate outcomes are determined by the levels and modes of combination of the many and various resource and non-resource inputs. *Final outcomes* are changes in users' welfare, ends in themselves, whereas *intermediate outcomes* are couched in terms of the means to those ends, such as providing care services or offering a supportive high quality residential environment. *Resource inputs* (summarised by costs) are defined as tangible items such as staff, buildings, provisions and other consumable items which go to create service packages. Resources are scarce, therefore we must make choices: economics examines choice under scarcity. *Non-resource inputs*, by contrast, are those determinants of final outcomes which are neither physical or tangible: they are embodied in the personalities, activities, attitudes and experiences of the main actors in the care system or process (Knapp, 1984).

The production of welfare framework has been used in research with almost every social care user group. This paper illustrates its potential in mental health care research.

The demands for cost information for mental health policy and practice are many. Costs data are required for bottom-up, needs-led multiple agency planning; for the development of 'affordable' community care plans; for care management, particularly where it is tied to devolved budgeting mechanisms; and for pricing, charging and contracting-out. Mental Illness Specific Grant applications require accurate costings and discussions during the PES rounds to decide the total MISG allocation. Furthermore, activities such as cost of illness studies, value-for-money auditing, performance reviews and evaluation of policies and practice all require a costs dimension in order to understand fully the consequences of decisions taken.

COSTS RESEARCH

The main purpose of this paper is illustrate some of the policy areas into which research can feed costs evidence and analysis. To do this I will allude to some research undertaken at the PSSRU. Elements of the research are only briefly described here and readers are urged to read the relevant papers to obtain the full context and flavour of these pieces of work. (Most references are to published work, but can also be obtained from the PSSRU.)

Research can take a broad view of the impact of policy decisions. To illustrate this I will use some data from work undertaken last year to examine the cost implications of providing care for elderly people with cognitive impairment. It is important that the cost implications are tracked across agency boundaries. In a research context this *comprehensive* perspective is becoming increasingly important as community care packages become more complex and varied. This is inevitable in a developing mixed economy with interventions aimed at more closely meeting individual need. In the real world comprehensive costs become more likely as care managers manoeuvre to organise appropriate care packages and as joint commissioning becomes a more common purchasing arrangement.

Our research examined the current balance of care for all elderly people with cognitive impairment in England (1991) using data on population size, accommodation and other service use. Costs were calculated for all settings and services. This in itself was a complex process. The research, however, went a stage further and located data on effective alternatives for care which were *also* comprehensively costed. These costed options allowed the examination of the resource implications of changing the balance of care to improve the quality of life for groups of elderly people. For example, we costed an improvement of respite care and better home-based support. Due mainly to the potential for relocation of the large number of people still resident in long-stay hospitals the research found overall savings could be made to the total cost of providing care. These savings accrued mainly to district health authorities and required greater levels of expenditure for some agencies, in particular, local authorities (Kavanagh, Schneider, Knapp, Beecham and Netten, 1993; Schneider, Kavanagh, Knapp, Beecham and Netten, 1993).

Getting information on services used by people and attaching costs are costly tasks. This is another area where research can help. First, it helps in the obvious and very general way. If the costing is done once it may not be necessary for everyone else to do it. *Unit Costs of Community Care 1992/93*, published by the PSSRU (Netten and Smart, 1993), is an example of the straightforward practical value of research. Research can also operate as *pathfinder* (or *path illuminator*) and reference point. For example, the enormous amount of PSSRU data on the costs of care for people with mental health problems has recently been examined to find a way of reducing the costs of costs research. Statistical analyses of these data suggest that close examination of receipt and calculation of costs of a *reduced list* of services (for example, accommodation, hospital services and day care) allowed accurate estimation of not less than 91 per cent of the total costs of care for people supported by community psychiatric nurses. Other reduced list calculations were conducted for other care arrangements and settings. Such short-cuts are of little use where comprehensive service receipt and costs data are required or where inter-individual variations in costs, needs or outcomes are of primary importance. Neither should they be used to set inflexible care budgets for individual clients. However, the reduced list methodology has the advantage of producing broad orders of magnitude for care costs for groups of users. Its adoption in appropriate areas could move us some distance towards enabling the demands for costs to be met by good quality data built on a solid research base (Knapp and Beecham, 1993).

However, we need to be careful with summary costs. They provide averages for groups of people, perhaps for whole populations. But research stresses the need and, thankfully, also offers the opportunity to *move beyond averages*, to examine individual variations. To an extent, a randomised control trial (RCT) obviates the need for such searching examination of data , but only if one is again concerned mainly with broad differences between policy or practice options. Obviously it is not possible to use this research design to study all issues.

The reprovision of services for long-stay hospital patients is an example of a policy where an RCT is not feasible and where we need to move beyond averages. Two psychiatric hospitals in the

North East Thames region (NETRHA) are the focus of an examination by the PSSRU of the costs and cost-effectiveness of services. The PSSRU research runs alongside a wide-ranging study of the impact of the service relocation (Leff, 1993). Currently, data on the comprehensive costs of community care are available for 341 former in-patients. The average cost of their care is £488 per week (1993 prices). The average cost of community care has risen as each annual cohort leaves hospital, but for only a third of the whole sample was hospital care more costly than community care. So, although the average cost of community care is less than hospital care it does not mean that community care *always* costs less than long-stay hospital care (Knapp, Beecham, Hallam and Fenyo, 1993).

The results from a more detailed examination of costs can further inform policy and planning. By combining data on community costs with data on needs and characteristics of sample members while in hospital, the costs of community care can be *predicted* for all long-stay hospital residents. Multivariate analysis showed the variation in the costs of community care could be explained in part by these data. Cost-raising factors are: gender (male); age; percentage of life spent in hospital; higher scores for non-specific neurotic syndrome and negative symptoms; greater numbers of staff in the patients' social networks; greater daily nursing requirements; and some aspects of social behaviour (Knapp et al., 1990). These results are useful for local planning for the closure of the two hospitals under study. Extrapolations from these results allowed community care costs to be predicted for all long-stay psychiatric hospital residents in North East Thames and also for all long-stay patients in England (Knapp, Beecham and Gordon, 1992). A more recent re-analysis of these cost predictions with a larger sample of people produced similar results (Knapp, Beecham, Fenyo and Hallam, 1994).

Having examined some of the areas in which costs data can inform policy and practice we can return to the production of welfare framework and examine the primary aim of community care — improving user welfare. Predicting costs is all very well, but what are the *effects* of the services (summarised by costs) on the people using them? The starting point is that costs may vary for a host of reasons, some of which have been noted already. Causes of variation may be: input prices; outcomes; occupancy; user characteristics; quality of care; social and physical environments; staffing levels and characteristics; location; sector of ownership; or efficiency. If these variations influences are looked at together we gain a valid picture of how user outcomes and costs are linked.

The results of analyses of costs, needs and outcomes data for the NETRHA study showed that variations in costs could be explained by a number of factors. Higher costs were found to be associated with *better outcomes* such as improvements in negative symptoms and general health, reduction in delusions and hallucinations, a broadening of social networks, but also with higher anxiety levels. Higher costs were also associated with *greater needs* as measured in terms of incontinence, mobility, affect, attitude to accommodation and community living skills. They were also associated with longer residence in hospital, marital status (single) and whether the client was socially withdrawn (Beecham, Knapp and Fenyo, 1991).

CONCLUSION

I hope this paper has demonstrated some of the valuable contributions which research can make to both policy and practice. But such research requires the observance of four principles. These are set out in chapter 5 of *Costing Community Care: Theory and Practice* (Netten and Beecham, 1993).
- Costs should be comprehensively measured.
- The costs variations inevitably revealed should be explored and exploited for valuable policy insights.
- Variations encourage comparisons, but only like-with-like comparisons have full validity.
- Cost information should be integrated where possible with information on client outcomes.

More importantly for those people who are not undertaking costs research but who are using the results, I would advocate scrutinising the research for observance of these four principles.

I hope and believe the fifth and final chapter in *The History of the Demand for Costs* will turn out to be the longest and richest in the book.

REFERENCES

Beecham, J.K., Knapp M.R.J. and Fenyo, A. (1991) Costs, needs and outcomes, *Schizophrenia Bulletin*, 17, 3, 427-439. This paper is also published in Netten, A. and Beecham, J. (eds) *Costing Community Care*, Ashgate, Aldershot, 1993.

Kavanagh, S., Schneider, J., Knapp, M.R.J., Beecham, J.K. and Netten, A. (1993) Elderly people with cognitive impairment: costing possible changes in the balance of care, *Health and Social Care in the Community*, 1, 69-80.

Knapp, M.R.J. (1984) *The Economics of Social Care*, Macmillan, London.

Knapp, M.R.J., and Beecham, J., (1993) Reduced-list costings: examination of an informed short-cut in mental health research, Discussion Paper 939, Personal Social Services Research Unit, University of Kent at Canterbury.

Knapp, M.R.J., Beecham, J.K., Anderson, J., Dayson, D., Leff, J., Margolius, O., O'Driscoll, C., and Wills, W., (1990) Predicting the community costs of closing psychiatric hospitals, *British Journal of Psychiatry*, 157, 661-70.

Knapp, M.R.J., Beecham, J.K. and Gordon, K. (1992) Predicting the community cost of closing psychiatric hospitals: National extrapolations, *Journal of Mental Health*, 1, 4, 315-326.

Knapp, M.R.J., Beecham, J., Hallam, A., Fenyo, A. (1993) The costs of community care for former long-stay psychiatric hospital patients, *Health and Social Care in the Community*, 1, 4, 193-201.

Knapp, M.R.J., Beecham, J.K., Fenyo, A. and Hallam, A. (1994) Predicting costs from needs and diagnoses: community mental health care for former hospital in-patients, *British Journal of Psychiatry*, 163, Supplement, forthcoming.

Leff, J. (ed.) (1993) The TAPS project: Evaluating community placement of long-stay psychiatric patients, *British Journal of Psychiatry*, 162, Supplement 19.

Netten, A. and Beecham, J. (eds) (1993) *Costing Community Care: Theory and Practice*, Ashgate, Aldershot.

Netten, A. and Smart, S. (1993) *Unit Costs of Community Care 1992/93*, PSSRU, Canterbury.

Schneider, J., Kavanagh, S., Knapp, M.R.J., Beecham, J.K. and Netten, A. (1993) Elderly people with advanced cognitive impairment in England: Resource use and costs, *Ageing and Society*, 13, 27-50.

Wistow, G., Knapp, M.R.J., Hardy, B. and Allen, C. (1994) *Social Care in a Mixed Economy*, Open University Press, Buckingham.

The problems presented in practice in local authorities

Mary Richardson
Director of Social Services, Waltham Forest

INTRODUCTION

As we use cost data in local authorities there are five important points to bear in mind.

Nothing is impossible
At present the agenda for change in local authorities seems almost endless, mammoth, and at times contradictory. Both politicians and staff would like to identify and hold on to some small anchors of certainty in the midst of the torrent of change. Developing a robust infrastructure with clear, understandable mechanisms to enable the management and organisation of work activity, is one way of providing the means for coherent policy and practice. Establishing precise costs is part of that activity. However, there is a myriad of problems in determining costs but, given time, there are solutions to them.

We must forget all ideas of steady state

One of the current difficulties for local government as a whole, is the major thrust away from a service providing function to an enabling function where authorities might not provide services at all. This dramatic political change has altered the fundamental purpose of local authorities: many of the debates taking place reflect the tensions between the traditional service providers and the new enablers. Although the backcloth for developing community care is a major political debate this is not just a policy difference between political parties. Additionally, community care is a dynamic process. Definitions of costs, therefore, will be refined and changed to meet changing priorities and ideas and as better structures and systems support becomes available.

We we can only do what we can do

None of us are starting with a blank sheet of paper; we have an existing agenda and tasks, and organisations with finite capacity. Changing complex structures and processes whilst continuing to meet user need removes many of the most radical options from use and there are inevitably compromises that have to be made.

More haste, less speed

We are not always able to travel to our destination by the most direct route. We have to avoid service dislocation for existing users: there are ongoing commitments to current service users and the need to run effective childcare services at the same time. The local authority infrastructure is vast and highly complex. There are hundreds, or even thousands, of inter-relating systems and procedures. Changing parts of these is not always straightforward and the outcomes of change are not always easy to foresee. Change needs to be worked out in every small detail if it is to operate successfully.

We must keep the user in view

There is not much point to all this change unless it benefits service users. Whilst determining costs properly has clear advantages for those who are not yet in the care system, for those who need to be maintained the advantage may be less obvious. A considerable amount of effort has to go into ensuring the impact of system change does not cause unnecessary uncertainty or confusion for users. Ultimately, having identifiable costs for all services provides the basis for reasonable, rational, consistent and cost-effective allocation to service users.

What are the problems? Some of those already alluded to in the introduction are discussed in more detail below. The first group of problems are those which affect the environment and the context of identifying costs. The second group relates to the particular difficulties in producing costs information.

THE COSTS ENVIRONMENT

'Supply-led' to 'needs-led' organisation

As already mentioned, community care is part of a wider political shift towards developing an 'enabling' role for local authorities, away from directly provided services. For community care that means politicians and managers will have less control over deciding what types of resources and facilities should be available and provided (in part) by the local authority in developing responsive and individually appropriate services.

The size and significance of this change should not be under-estimated. In the traditional model, information about costs was comparatively unimportant. Each social services authority would provide certain services for the different care groups. Politicians would be proud of their services and they were regarded as evidence of civic achievement and commitment to the local population. When financial crises came there would be scrutiny of what was being spent and this might result, for example, in decisions about paring the food bills of an old people's home, or having economy drives with heating and lighting or, in drastic cases, a closure of a whole facility. But in general, there was no focus on detailed information about costs, and only very rarely a look at the comparative costs of services.

Determining what resources ought to be allocated to an individual user would largely be decided by the availability of known resources and facilities. No price tag was associated with this activity. 'Gatekeeping' to services happened mostly by denying access to assessment in a variety of ways. The effect of this was inconsistent decision-making and often differential service provision for people in similar need living in the same neighbourhood, let alone between different local authorities. Meeting the new agenda, therefore, requires a large cultural shift in jobs, roles and staff attitudes in social services departments.

There is a re-training issue for staff at all levels and all types. In the past, staff skills have been developed in designing, managing and running services in which costs did not play the same function as now required. Today, managers in directly provided services have to compete for business in a market-place. In the past managers would have been selected for their care and staff management skills, now they must be selected also for their financial and entrepreneurial ones. Assessment and commissioning staff must be able to design packages of care within prescribed resource parameters.

No-one should minimise how basic these shifts are and how they undermine previously held values of politicians and staff. There are different ways managers can assist the processes of change in different local authorities depending on political circumstances. One bottom line for authorities wishing to retain their existing services, is that successful competition relies on provision of services which have been chosen by users and which are competitively priced. This requires detailed cost information which in turn requires new systems and procedures for budgets.

Getting staff to shift to the new mode overnight is impossible. In the past, many social workers have been reluctant to undertake financial assessments on service users let alone keep detailed records of the costs of services provided. Dividing these tasks into manageable parts helps the move forward, for example, working out schedules of service units by cost. The need for training in the new areas of work is self-evident and easy to state but never easy to achieve for the large number of staff who require it.

Demands other than community care on the social services department
The size of the work agenda, apart from the massive community care one, is considerable. For example, there is white collar compulsory competitive tendering (CCT), substantial new health and safety legislation, the reshaping of children's services under the Children Act and the implications of the Criminal Justice Act. These are overlaid by other political agendas for each individual local authority.

A number of these developments, at least theoretically, fit well with the requirements to produce cost information for community care. Whilst community care does not include legislative compulsion to compete for whole services, personal social services and directly provided services will ultimately face similar imperatives. But because of these other tasks the difficulties in producing cost information for community care are essentially two-fold. First, community care is not necessarily the top priority for everyone in social services or the council. This is a critical point, as some staff outside the community care arena may have key roles in changing the infrastructure and producing cost information for that purpose. Second, some of these other work areas may conflict with or complicate the community care task. New areas subject to CCT include personnel, finance, information technology, and information and publicity services. How and where the service boundaries are determined and how they are subjected to tendering can have a direct impact on unit costs for social services.

Differences between social services and finance departments
The stories of difficulties between theses two are legion. In my experience, the problems do not arise because the staff of either department are nasty or unpleasant. There are real differences because of different priorities and different values. Traditionally, the director of finance is believed to have thought the council's monies were his. These sorts of views, even if they once prevailed, have been radically affected by the development of corporate management, new fiscal duties and the advent of CCT. However, the finance department still prioritises collecting money over spending money.

Responsibility for public accountability for expenditure sits uneasily with flexible service patterns and devolved budget responsibilities. Finance departments, if they are not committed to the new approaches, will not be very helpful in assisting with developing proper unit costs so new systems can be set up.

The organisational structures of many finance departments still reflect traditional local authority budget management where the shape and direction of staff activity is towards meeting global requirements supported by mainframe computing. These structures are good for producing annual accounts and for meeting formal static requirements retrospectively, but do not help to develop the up-to-the-minute cost information that is essential for changing and flexible services.

In such a large system, three factors contribute to the conflict between finance and social services staff: the time delay in producing information on a mainframe computer; the inevitable errors resulting from data entry undertaken at a considerable distance from the activity; and the different systems of accounting which invariably seem to exist.

PRODUCING COSTS DATA

Difficulties in defining costs
Researchers have taken a book to set out different ways of defining costs so there is no need to apologise for saying this is a real problem in practice. Without detailing the various types of costs it suffices to say that in community care rarely, if ever, do the non-social services costs feature in the equation. Only recently has there been some consideration of the associated health costs, and only recently have we seen the start of joint commissioning. These developments, even with every authority having an agreement about continuing care beds, rarely use detailed cost information.

The need which social services departments have to define costs is limited to maximising the use of the monies already allocated to it. In practice, there may be a further limitation to establishing costs only for services provided. In the long term, it would be helpful to establish the true costs of the assessment and commissioning services. Additionally, there are a range of departmental and corporate costs which ought to be apportioned. The current organisation of all these activities is likely to militate against real allocations. Moreover, before costs can be defined, activity levels have to be defined. Workload measurement systems are not common in social services, and much time is being spent introducing them.

Essentially, it is important to start with what is possible, and that which provides reliable data for care packaging. It is conceivable that in just dealing with the immediate costs of service provision decisions based on comparative costs will be erroneous. However, in my judgement, the work involved in the additional task of properly including indirect costs is so great that the time could not be justified at present.

There are also a range of ordinary book-keeping problems in defining costs. The simple question 'What is the right figure?' is one that has to be asked all the time. The laborious local authority processes of income receipt and paying bills hinder the processes of accounting. In practice, so many people may be involved that unless precise definitions are used, variations will creep in by themselves. The need to define time frames is important too: costs over one year might be very different than costs over five years. Accountancy is an art not a science and there are many ways of cutting the costs cake.

Problems in setting the agenda for establishing costs
First, if the priority is to purchase packages of care in the most effective and efficient way, then we need to determine equivalence between different services. This equivalence is required between the different units of in-house services *and* those provided externally. Though there has been a long-standing comprehensive use of the private and voluntary sectors by social services departments, the introduction of contracts based on a specification with agreed costs is very new. In the past, services were purchased to meet specific needs that were not met in-house and there was little reference to cost. Where costs were discussed they were total not unit costs and any negotiations would be at the margin.

This equivalence can only be achieved by service specification which should include the precise relationship between the unit selected and the criteria for providing services. In reality, the mechanisms for achieving this are not well developed in either the independent or statutory sectors. The costs of managing monitoring and evaluation systems need to be included and may be more expensive for external contracts. Social services departments also have risks to manage which are very difficult to fit into the cost equation. They need to ensure there is a mixed economy of care and that where there are failures in the private and voluntary sectors, there is service provision for vulnerable people.

In the local authority context, the role of 'on-costs' will become critical, as it has for previous services subjected to CCT. The in-house service providers want a level playing field with their private and voluntary counterparts and there are issues raised in many authorities about whether social services have been unfairly saddled with 'on-costs' because of CCT elsewhere. However, there has to be some agreement about corporate or departmental activity which would exist, and the level to which it would exist, regardless of whether there were in-house services or not.

Systems and structures — or the lack of them

There are four problems here. First we have organisational shapes that are geared to hierarchy and the previous requirements of public service. The answer is not simply about developing a purchaser/provider split, useful though this may be in this context. It is also about being able to define the different functional parts of staff's activities where these tend to be multi-faceted and transferring responsibilities so that new systems can work. It may be that staff responsible for financial assessments and charges should be functionally related to the running of services.

Second, many of the accounting methods and practices still relate to the traditional way of balancing the books retrospectively. There have been no systems of commitment accounting until recently. As budgets have been devolved, and service areas have been responsible for their own accounts, reconciling them with the formal, mainframe system has been difficult and time-consuming. There have been no immediate ways of looking at expenditure against budget, changing service patterns, or examining the basis for detailed costing on actual spend.

Third, many of the difficulties raised above have been directly affected by inappropriate (or non-existent) information technology. Introducing technology to meet the new requirements is made the more difficult by the lack of experience and skill in operating these systems.

Finally, there are always problems with data processing in large organisations where it is usual for several people to handle each item. The likelihood of mistakes caused by poor data transfer or lack of commitment to the task is high.

Skills, knowledge and experience

This relates to the the training and development deficit in producing financial information and using it. There are many issues about how budget-holding can be devolved and managed. Many of us have been devolving budgets for some time, particularly in the areas of direct service provision. My department is not alone in finding that the staff most experienced and competent in financial management are not in the assessment and commissioning areas where purchasing responsibilities ultimately should be. This skills deficit is one that can only be remedied over time. Hybrid and transitional arrangements are often necessary to ensure public accountability for new

The problems presented in practice in local authorities 35

funds and to maximise the use of them by applying existing knowledge and skills.

The enormity of the new task of ensuring the new community care requirements are met has meant that staff have needed much information and specific training. To avoid overwhelming staff most authorities have accepted that the transition has to be gradual.

SOLUTIONS (AS OPPOSED TO CONCLUSIONS)

There are ways forward to resolve the difficulties experienced.

First, senior managers have a key role in facilitating the various shifts which need to be made. Clearly the way in which each authority wishes to organise its in-house provision will be different. What they will have in common is the need for proper cost information, regardless of political ends. Briefing politicians about the changing responsibilities of social services departments is a continuous process. Continuing to provide staff with information, training and support are crucial. There is a need to emphasise that unit costs information is necessary to encourage adaptability and efficiency in the current system, and that it is a means to future survival.

Second, for managers, there is no substitute for steady, methodical work to a pre-organised and timetabled plan. This has been described as 'project management' and requires going back to basics and unpicking every item, especially in those authorities where there are no pre-existing discrete service budgets. The use of proformas and schedules is very helpful in this work. By way of a plug for our Kent sponsors today, having something which, at worst, you can tear apart always helps to move the process on.

Third, departments must take on the new management responsibilities gradually. There is a need to give all the detailed work around costs some meaning so the task is tackled with enthusiasm. For example, setting quality standards with performance measurement as a basis for marketing in-house services, gives a focus to establishing cost information. However radical the ultimate plans, paths have to be found to enable the organisation to continue to function whilst change takes place.

Common issues — costs in health and social services

Chris Gostick
Community Care Manager, North West Thames Regional Health Authority

INTRODUCTION

It is important to be clear that costs data are not ends in themselves, but essential components in the process of improving the relationship between needs, resources and outcomes. It is equally important to recognise that the best measures of outcomes are in terms of improved services or experiences for clients, patients or other users, not in any simple quantitative indicator.

Simply holding this conference represents an emerging recognition of the increasing importance of cost data in the overall process of developing more effective health and social care services, but it is useful to be reminded of the distinction between costs and prices as set out in chapter 4 of *Costing Community Care: Theory and Practice*. My previous involvement with local authority finance directors has indicated a distinct emphasis on prices rather than costs, and I recognise similar features in the NHS. Martin Knapp remarks:

Public sector accounts are designed for budgeting and financial probity, and it is not therefore surprising that they provide an inadequate basis for costing services. (Knapp, 1993, p.15)

Ever the tactful researcher! Just enough truth to satisfy the harassed practitioner or manager; not enough to disturb the equanimity of local authority finance directors. For myself, I would wish to be a little stronger, and to emphasise the continued dominance of bureaucratic centralism and control in both health and social services, largely based on the ownership of expensive central computer systems, and the control of information.

Nonetheless, it is equally important to recognise that new developments such as the local management of schools (LMS), the community care reforms, and in its own way the introduction of compulsory competitive tendering (CCT) in local government, have provided valuable levers for operational senior managers within local authorities to push back the boundaries. However, the battle is as yet far from won.

Joint commissioning

Full implementation of the NHS and community care reforms requires far more effective integration of health and local authority activities than ever before. There are encouraging signs that this is happening, but in his paper Martin Knapp clearly showed the importance of identifying the full costs of those services that cross individual agency financial boundaries, and the potential risk of the introduction of perverse incentives to off-load responsibility for expensive services onto other agencies.

One of the most effective methods for achieving closer working and better integration appears to be within the general framework of joint commissioning. I recognise that this still means many different things to different people, and I do not intend to initiate a debate on the issue here, but the approach does provide a useful framework in which to consider some important common issues. I would particularly commend the recent Department of Health publication *Joint Commissioning — A Slice Through Time* (1993), as an important contribution to that debate. The document suggests that:

The heart of joint commissioning is the development of compatible or single service specifications and contracts for specified services, locations, volume, costs and quality. (DH, 1993, p. 21).

The report outlines in detail the processes involved in joint commissioning, and identifies the four essential inputs to that process. These are worth referring to here:

- *Good practice research.* This appears to be a good opportunity to tell researchers and research funders to try even harder. Whilst we now know a good deal more about the relationship between needs, resources and outcomes than we did only four or five years ago, we still have far too little information on how to achieve the most effective social care responses from the range of resources available. More work in this area is urgently needed if we are to address this imbalance.
- *Needs assessment.* This area is beginning to improve rapidly, but there are still some general difficulties that need to be addressed when integrating the range of data being generated by different agencies.
- *Provider information.* This is also improving, but inevitably from a very low baseline. We now have much better 'maps' of available services beginning to emerge, but there is still far too little information on provider quality or performance, or on the relationship between costs and prices.
- *Financial information.* This is critical for us today. Despite a good deal of attention over the past few years this area is still severely deficient in good reliable information that can be used for both strategic commissioning purposes on the one hand, and for effective care management, or micro-purchasing, on the other.

You will have your own views on the reliability and effectiveness of your local information. My experience in North West Thames and elsewhere suggests that information quality is now improving in all major agencies, but probably still too slowly. So far the handful of second year Community Care Plans I have seen support this general view. Whilst there are significant improvements on the original plans in terms of focus, there are still problems over both the inclusion and presentation of information. Financial information tends still to be presented in the global sense of total agency or service budgets. In particular, too often there is a separation of the resource data provided by each of the key agencies, and too little information on the actual costs of services. This may, of course, just be a presentational problem and the source data may be available, but somehow I doubt it.

These problems are hardly surprising. We are all aware of the major difficulties of obtaining better quality information, and the first requirement is to be much clearer about what information we need, and how we will use it when we have it. For this alone *Costing Community Care* and the complementary booklet *Unit Costs of Community Care 1992/1993* (Netten and Smart, 1993) are to be welcomed.

COLLATING INFORMATION

Whilst there is no doubt that individual authorities, whether local authority social services departments, health authorities, family health services authorities or voluntary organisations, are now much better at collecting and manipulating their own operational and financial data, the real problems emerge in trying to bring this information together within the joint commissioning framework at a local level. I don't need to dwell on these difficulties at length, but some are sufficiently important to be worth stressing again.

- We still have no *standardised definitions*, particularly in relation to services, clients, patients and activities (most especially the distribution of overheads, on-costs and other central or departmental charges), and some central guidance on this issue from the Department of Health or the Audit Commission would be invaluable. The need for a standardised minimum national indicator set is now overwhelming.
- The good news on *population co-terminosity* is the increasing development of health commissioning agencies with largely co-terminous health and local authority boundaries. However, we need to recognise the growing importance of GPs, especially fundholding GPs. This brings in a whole new set of problems, as GP practice catchments frequently cross FHSA, health authority and local authority area boundaries. This has been clearly demonstrated in a collaborative commissioning project in North East Westminster, which has identified 55 GPs with patients in the geographic area of North East Westminster itself, but by no means all of these GPs are actually located within the area itself, whilst those GPs within the area often have many of their patients outside the area. In future it will be important to be much clearer about the catchment area of the populations to which individual agencies are relating. GP/FHSA data is probably the best starting point for developing locally integrated client/patient information

systems.
- As clients/patients pass through the various health and social care systems, they also pass through individual agency information systems. Whilst social services are now much better at *client identification* — who gets which services and when — this now needs to be widened to a multi-agency approach, possibly by the use of some form of common identifier for individual clients, to be used by all agencies.
- There are still major problems over confidentiality and data exchange and data protection requirements. These can only be resolved by clear inter-agency agreements. *Incompatible data processing systems* compound these difficulties. Many social services systems are still operating as part of larger corporate local authority information systems which make improved links with health agency systems difficult to achieve even though these health links may be more appropriate.
- *Commercial sensitivity* is becoming a real problem when trying to collate information. There is increasing evidence to suggest that some NHS Trusts and private sector providers are reluctant to provide data on costs and prices because of the possible use of this data by their competitors.
- Again, I don't need to dwell on the issue of *charges*. NHS services continue to be free at the point of delivery, whilst local authorities are increasingly being required to generate increased income through the use of charges. This inevitably makes it difficult to provide integrated seamless services of the sort required by the community care reforms.

These are just some of the problems that need to be jointly addressed at the local level if more effective information systems are to be achieved. Increasingly I tend to the view that the achievement of fully integrated local systems is a long way off, and that for the present we should continue to maintain individual agency systems, but with as many common features as possible, with a gradual move towards greater convergence. This could be best facilitated by the introduction of some form of common information currency or rate of exchange, similar to the European Currency Unit (ECU) concept, to link individual agency cost data and financial systems together, for use by individual joint commissioning teams.

So far joint commissioning developments have only really involved health and social services agencies looking at their own information systems, with some help from voluntary sector coordinating groups. There is still a need to engage more effectively with the independent sector, especially private providers, and to be much clearer about data requirements — in particular cost, price and through-put information. This is not particularly an issue of commercial sensitivity. Often these types of data are simply not available in a useable form so it will be important to begin to establish clear local guidelines for data required from providers. This must be done soon as there is already evidence of rapid diversification of the private sector from the existing concentration on residential care into new services and new markets.

Finally, the crucial importance of users and carers in the process of planning and developing service specifications and commissioning plans must not be overlooked.

CONCLUSION

Despite the seemingly insurmountable difficulties, there is already reassuring evidence of progress; both improved individual agency information systems, and increased integration of those systems as a way of improving cost data. The essential requirements of progress seem to be:

- *Clarity of purpose.* Identification of what needs to be done, by whom and when.
- *Leadership.* Without commitment from chief officers and elected members it is likely nothing will be achieved.
- *Project management.* This requires clear responsibility to a named manager with sufficient time and influence to progress the various stages of the programme.
- *Involvement* of finance and information staff from all agencies in the wider joint commissioning activities, so they can see how their information is used and why accuracy and reliability are so important.
- *Innovation.* Consistently we need to think the unthinkable, and to look for new approaches to old problems.
- *External facilitation.* It sometimes helps to have an external person available to ask awkward questions, and to bring new perspectives and ideas.

Finally, there is nothing like some success to help celebrate the efforts of those involved, and to reinvigorate the process. So start small and achieve targets more rapidly.

It will inevitably be a long and difficult process. But first steps are always the hardest, and these have already been taken. We need now to keep the process going. We are engaged in a joint collaborative exercise, not just between health and local authorities and other provider agencies, but in a process of continual improvement and reflection in which academics, researchers and central policy makers must also engage. All have important contributions to make, and the work of the PSSRU and similar units should provide the essential framework within which that collaboration can occur.

REFERENCES

Department of Health (1993) *Joint Commissioning — A Slice Through Time*, HMSO, London.

Knapp, M.R.J. (1993) 'Background Theory', in Netten and Beecham (eds) *Costing Community Care: Theory and Practice*, Ashgate, Aldershot.

Netten, A. and Beecham, J. (eds) (1993) *Costing Community Care: Theory and Practice*, Ashgate, Aldershot.

Netten, A. and Smart, S. (1993) *Unit Costs of Community Care 1992/1993*, PSSRU, Canterbury.

Approaches to compiling and using cost information

David Claridge
Assistant Director of Adult Social Services, Croydon

INTRODUCTION

In the last twelve months I have spent half my time with the Community Care Support Force. It gave me a unique opportunity to visit a large number of authorities as well as exchange information with colleagues on the Support Force who visited other authorities. The Support Force was able to assemble a pretty good picture of community care implementation. It is true that there are some leading-edge players, but very few, if any, social service departments or district health authorities have got all aspects of implementation taped — even if they would have you believe that to be the case. It is the connection of rhetoric with reality that I want to talk about today and the methodology for achieving it.

Of course it's dangerous to generalise but my perceptions from the Support Force experience is that in the run up to 1st April 1993 the preoccupation has been entirely on external costs — that is independent sector costs. Some authorities are setting an arbitrary cost limit for the price of residential and nursing care, others are doing so following a tendering exercise. Virtually all authorities are setting their usual price without regard to the cost of their own residential accommodation. In fact, some social service departments do not know what that cost is. They may have a method for calculating the charge for 'Part III' accommodation but that is not necessarily the same thing. A further factor is that many social service departments have built up knowledge and skills about budget management, contracting, and the like at the centre, but not done anything substantial about transferring these skills to operational managers or to the people expected to make decisions in a timely fashion — care managers.

I think there are two principal reasons for this failure to devolve responsibility. First, it is thought to be much easier to control any large organisation by holding key decisions at the centre. Second, and I think by far the most significant of the two, is that without a clear vision expressed about the goal to be achieved *and* a project management approach to take you there, progress is left to happenstance. In consequence progress is often stalled before achieving any momentum.

The message I want to put across today is that the ground to be covered is vast and unless an incremental approach to developing expertise is established which is shared within a department or authority it is likely to come to grief. A long-term game plan should be developed and the necessary steps determined. Clarity of leadership is essential although the participants should be all the key operational players.

COST CENTRES IN CROYDON

I'd like to describe what we are doing in Croydon. Not because we are necessarily a centre of excellence, but because I think we are pretty much part of the mainstream of social services departments.

The foundation stones for change were laid several years ago when we moved to cost centre budgeting. Instead of lumping all our expenditure together by function, we split initially into some 200 cost centres, now increased to nearly 300. This enabled us to separately identify the cost of every establishment, team or sub-team within the department. The annual budget cycle has been an iterative process that has enabled us to refine our approach.

Like many authorities, we used the CIPFA PSS statistics and key indicator material to compare ourselves with other, broadly similar, social service departments. However, the detailed analysis that we could obtain from our cost centre based information enabled us to take a deeper look at ourselves.

Over the years, for example, we have used cost centre based information to identify which Part III homes should close, which buildings to target first for energy efficiency measures and to deal with budget pressure points. It was also an essential source of information when we were asked to consider proposals to form a trust around ten social services residential homes for elderly people. In the end we did not proceed because we predicted costs would increase. (Some of you may have seen the recent *Care Weekly* article on trusts created by social services highlighting the uncertainties of the territory.) This is not to say that cost centre accounting is the be all and end all. We still have to maintain control over residential placements budgets through commitment accounting systems that are separate to our main financial information system. However, in terms of sharpening the quality of information and managerial accountability, a cost centre based approach is an essential foundation on which to build. Moreover, it is essential to ensure that accountability is transferred to budget managers who are trained and who are equipped with the information to enable them to manage.

CARE MANAGEMENT

Just over two years ago we formed the view that care managers would, from 1st April 1993, cost the packages of care they developed. Our reasons for this were four-fold. First, it would begin to bring our own costs more clearly into the frame. Second, over time, care managers' decisions could be exercised in a climate of greater freedom, although guidance would be given in terms of maximum costs for packages of community based services. (For example, we would not usually expect to spend more on a recurring basis to maintain someone at home than if they were accommodated in a nursing or residential home.) Third, the process would ensure that care managers were grounded in some sense of resource reality and that users and carers were not given false expectations. Fourth, users and carers would increasingly have a clearer idea of the value of care packages that were enabling users to remain living at home.

To underpin our approach we've developed information technology systems that enable care managers to cost the care package and, no doubt like many other departments, our ultimate goal is to commit expenditure on the basis of the final approved care package for each user through a link to the financial information system.

UNIT COSTS

Our work on establishing the unit costs of in-house services only began about a year ago. Some of it was not finished until this February. In the last two years we have changed from a central establishment charge which apportioned costs to client groups based on the budget size and nothing else. Significantly, local management of schools and compulsory competitive tendering (CCT) legislation has developed the centrally based skills and systems in local authorities to enable meaningful overhead costs (other than the departments own overheads) to be established.

The unit costs care managers are using to cost packages of care showed marked difference between long and short stay care, due of course, to the low maximum occupancy in short-stay services, about 75 per cent as opposed to over 90 per cent for long stay. Using designated beds rather than any vacancy that might exist may not be cost-efficient but raises qualitative issues that we felt were significant enough to pursue. We did so initially without examining cost implications although now we have this data we will consider whether the increased cost is value for money.

Of course, our exercise to establish more accurate unit costs gave us a few surprises. For example, I had not expected the cost of maintaining one hour of home care service to be quite as much as £9.68, even though I had felt our previously quoted hourly rate (for charging purposes) was rather low at £5.88 for a full cost payer. Whilst it seems perfectly sensible to strive for more accurate unit costs it does throw into the spotlight the implications for charging policies. Like the majority of social service departments we have not overhauled our charging policy in time for April 1993. Apart from the sheer complexity of developing an equitable set of charging arrangements (as opposed to income generating ones) for day and domiciliary services, the timing of its implementation is of critical significance. In London, for instance, any time before May 1994 may not be an op-

Approaches to compiling and using cost information

portune time to ask members to agree a policy which is likely to result in higher charges for domiciliary services for those who have the means to pay.

We have got part way there by gaining committee approval for what we think are more realistic unit costs, supplemented by devices to protect payer-users and a recognition that calculating unit costs will be a skill gained over time. For example, our maximum charge for home care in 1993/94 is £6.00 (after adding 2 per cent inflation to the 1992/93 level) but the new policy recognises that the social services department subsidises users by a minimum of 38 per cent and a maximum of 100 per cent for the majority of users who are on income support.

There were two reasons for wanting to bring our own costs more sharply into focus. The first was to ensure that purchasers (care managers, their team and senior managers) began to make serious comparisons between the costs they were paying for in-house services and those paid to or bid by independent sector providers. The second was to begin to create a much greater appreciation, indeed a passion, about costs in the various levels of provider management.

The development of a managerial passion about costs may be seen as unnecessary (or worse still, unhealthy) by some observers. I think it is vital for survival. Even though there is no CCT in the social care world at present, there is plenty of evidence that some social service departments are willing to put most, if not all, of their services outwith their direct control. Westminster is the latest authority to take this course. The question is how quickly will the rest of us follow, either through tendering, trust creation or both.

As I said earlier, in the run-up to 1st April most social service departments have been pre-occupied with coming to terms with purchasing from the independent sector. Many departments have ignored their own costs (if they know them with any accuracy) for the purposes of setting bench mark or 'usual' prices. It's only a matter of time, especially as resources become ever more stretched, before purchasers will want to put in-house costs under the microscope in a more challenging way than previous comparisons (using CIPFA and SSI materials) have done.

By developing a passion about costs in directly managed provider services we should be able to create more freedom for unit managers. I am advocating a sort of LMSS: a locally managed social services where individual establishments have much greater autonomy to respond to the purchasers' specification and have much less control from the centre. This will promote genuine liberation and not a sham arrangement that still requires the centre to sanction innovation. It is not, therefore, about developing a passion for the cheapest possible options with no regard to quality. It is about having the freedom to organise staff and other resources that will enable a cost-effective service to be delivered. For those departments that do not intend to put their in-house services out to tender immediately, incremental development of skills and movement toward more freedom to operate cost-effectively ought to occur. I would emphasise my earlier comment that this does not mean a development free-for-all, but development within a clear framework that has a vision of the end state. There is a host of issues to tackle systematically — ranging from charges to procedures, to training programmes.

In Croydon, 1993/94 to 1994/95 is the timeframe we envisage for developing provider manager skills. This includes reconsidering all current organisational relationships, procedures and training. For example, who manages the administration staff? Where do training budgets sit? How much in-house management overhead do you really need to run a service effectively? It is fair to say that this is more likely to be a parallel development phase for both purchasers and providers, rather than a one-sided programme.

There are, however, critical differences between the two halves of the programme. On the *purchasing side* more explicit quality measures must be developed to accompany the stated volume of purchasing. We have a long way to go in this respect. We need some idea of what a level of quality will cost. The end state will be an imaginative, comprehensively costed purchasing plan. On the *provider side* we must cost every aspect of activity that creates the service provided and that meets the quality standards specified. There will be no room for getting it wrong. In the private sector, that would mean going bust, in the public sector it still means an overspend. The question is, how much longer will that be a legitimate option for the public sector. A few social service departments have ostensibly implemented a survive-or-die policy for their in-house providers. In the short term it remains to be seen whether this is a real policy or a cosmetic one. In the medium term, it is inevitably going to become a real one.

CONCLUSION

So what is important in compiling and using cost information? I think it is the application of costing in a clear context that is not just single project orientated. For me, it starts with a vision of *who* will need to use the information and *how* it will be used — and the incremental steps that will take you to the achievement of the vision. These steps will include tackling: skills deficits; attitude; information; organisational boundaries; and commitment. The vision will need to be underpinned by a project plan with a project management approach, training and a passion to see it through.

Performance measurement and value for money

David Browning
Associate Director for Health and Social Service Studies, Audit Commission

INTRODUCTION

Costing is becoming increasingly important — not because of the pre-eminence of accountants, but because of the fundamental shifts away from a service-based to a user-centred approach which moves money closer to users. Funding services directly (the traditional approach) has tended to produce an inflexible form of care. Pushing funds closer to users is intended to provide more flexible services for users and their carers and this is the reason we are focusing on costs and financial management.

We will not be able to redirect funds straight away, pulling money away from existing services, diverting it to care managers and telling them to get on and spend it how they like. That would be a recipe for chaos. We must be well organised in how we move to a user-centred approach.

THE ROLE OF COSTS

Costs will prove useful in the quest for greater flexibility at two levels: at the operational level and at the strategic level. At the *operational level*, the care manager carries out the assessment and then, if the user meets the eligibility criteria, assembles a package of care, taking account of the cost of each service. This is why costs are important — not to make services more efficient (although this is important), but to allow users to choose combinations of services that meet their needs within a budget devolved to care managers. This sort of approach will be a long way off, and we will need to proceed with caution.

Costs are also needed at the *strategic level*. Most authorities will need to go through a systematic review of what they are about if they are to provide the sort of services that we all want to see. They will need to identify who needs support and how many of them there are. They will need to set priorities, and then apply costs to work out how much in total is required to meet people's needs in the numbers expected. They must then compare the total with the budget and loop back, adjusting priorities until both are brought into some sort of relationship. Priorities should then give clear eligibility criteria, and determine the amounts of money that the authority can make available for different types of people. Again, it will take a long time to put this sort of 'needs-based budgeting' process into place and money will continue to be locked up in services for the immediate future. But eventually an approach of this type will be needed, again requiring cost information.

So costing is about setting the strategies and the packages of care for individual users — very much at the heart of the new approach — and not about 'trimming the flab'. However, once costs have been identified and compared, it will be possible to identify the inefficient services, and make adjustments as necessary.

APPROACHES TO COSTING PROBLEMS

Another message which emerges from this volume is that *costs are slippery*. At the Commission we have been trying to work out whether money has been moving away from mental health services as the long stay hospitals have closed. We have found that the critical factor is the cost inflator used in the calculations. In the case of capital, a different figure may be needed depending on whether a resource is being bought or sold — producing a 'kinked' cost curve.

So costs are complex and difficult to work out. But they are relatively simple compared with measuring outcomes and needs. To analyse value for money we need to relate costs to needs and outcomes. The greater the needs, the higher the costs for the same outcome; or if you cut costs, your outcomes may go down for the same needs. Trying to develop a system that will relate these three things is extremely difficult. In Wales, the Commission is helping to develop an approach which relates outcomes and costs, as part of the review of the All Wales Strategy for people with a learning disability. But the outcomes require about seventy measures, even for a strategy which has a limited number of clear objectives. Some of the work done in the PSSRU specifying outcomes is similarly complex. Relating outcomes to dependency groups adds another layer of complexity.

Against this background, those in local authorities must start or continue the process of costing. It would be unfortunate if the only message from this conference were that everything is very difficult. There are many practical steps that can be taken. There is much helpful CIPFA guidance available that will help in the construction of preliminary costs now, while still recognising that the total picture is complex. It is possible to start sorting out how to put the cost components together to give total costs — components such as staff, materials, capital and overheads. We must agree on conventions that allow costs to be generated that are comparable between authorities, and CIPFA has given a strong lead here.

A key aspect of the changes is the commissioner/provider split. Without it, money cannot be moved closer to users. It also helps resolve the problem of overheads, which can be divided between commissioning overheads (for example council meetings) and provider overheads (for example payroll for staff). Where staff work for both, their time must be apportioned between commissioning and providing. In this way internal provider overheads can be generated comparable with those of the independent sector. Capital also needs some extra thought. It cannot be based on debt charges. Instead real values must be used, and most authorities are valuing their capital assets to provide the basis for the new ways of capital accounting.

By beginning to construct such basic rules we can start to map out costs which mean something. We shall need to get more sophisticated over time but we can start slowly.

This summer, the Audit Commission will be monitoring the special transitional grant. It is the one source of funds that is not already attached to services, and most of it (85 per cent) must be spent as purchasing non-local authority services. Here is a perfect vehicle for us to start to develop a costing approach in a modest way for in-house services in order to compare them with prices in the independent sector. We can also see how contracts are being met and finance controlled — giving a relatively small scale 'test bed' for the new approach, using cost information in a constructive way. This is a good way to start and will take us forward in incremental steps.

CONCLUSION

Costing is not done for its own sake, but as a basic building block for the new approach to community care which should lead to a better service for users. The key to good costing is clarity — clarity of thought about what we want, as in the All Wales Strategy. We must be pragmatic in the short term, producing costs that make sense, enabling us to come up with something we can work with. We have to start trying the approach out in a small way initially, linked to the special transitional grant, for example. We need to take it gradually, working towards a more sophisticated approach in a programmed way.

In this way, we can progress steadily, always keeping the goal of better services for users as our guide.

Messages of the day

Jennifer Bernard
General Manager Community Care, Birmingham Social Services
(now Director, Newcastle Social Services)

A constant theme in all the contributions to this conference has been the dramatic increase in interest in costs, particularly from local government officers. Of course this reflects the realities of managing in a much more competitive environment, with central government determined to open public services to greater scrutiny. But to think it *only* reflected that would be unduly cynical. I feel that the obligation to offer a greater choice of service to users and their carers has been grasped because it fits with the philosophy of care that underpins public sector work. You cannot extend choice and locate directly-managed services in a competitive world without taking a keen interest in costs, their derivation and how to use them in constructive comparison.

As part of the business planning approach which is becoming an integral part of providing a service, provider staff and their managers will have to take account of cost data and how it is made up. There will be a ripple effect as they challenge local authority procedures on purchasing, buildings maintenance and personnel practice in search of better value. Unit autonomy will have to be balanced with corporate interests and the proper auditing of public funds.

Care management and commissioning staff will want to take account of cost data to make the optimum choice of service available to the user and carer. They too will have regard both for the corporate effect of decisions taken, and for financial probity. As David Claridge explained, senior managers will have to ensure that the balance between competition and cooperation is struck in managing relationships so that quality is part of the picture.

In all agencies, senior managers may be tempted to engage in cost shunting between departments or between parts of the welfare state. Analysis of the distribution of funds from health programmes to reprovide long-stay hospital facilities will become urgent, for example. The boundaries between health and social care will be patrolled. Joint commissioning, leading to joint purchasing, must continue to be developed, as Chris Gostick urged. Skill mix must not be neglected.

Data on cost also matters because, by shaping commissioning and influencing the pattern of provision, their use will affect the choice of service available to users and their carers. As Clive Smee reminded us, costs information will inevitably become a powerful tool in policy-making. It is not being dramatic to recognise that cost data will have a part to play in determining the operation of the welfare state, as cost comparisons between providers and types of service give powerful messages to national and local politicians and the public.

To quote David Browning, 'costs are slippery things'. In this context, the accountant's answer to the question 'what is two plus two?' is worth remembering: 'What sort of number did you have in mind?'. The importance of a responsible use of such data cannot be overstated. It is easy, for example, to compare the costs of residential care or domiciliary support made available from the local authority, the voluntary sector and the private sector and conclude that because the local authority's costs are highest (as would almost certainly be the case) those services should not be used. Such a simplistic approach ignores the different conventions from which public costs have been built and the context for those costs. Ken Wright warned of the dangers of uncritical reliance on less than perfect data. We must remember too the transaction costs to the public sector of being an enabler. Those contracting and monitoring costs have to reappear somewhere in the analysis of accounts.

Without dwelling on the implications of under-using capital investment or the role of democratically elected politicians in making policy decisions about the balance of provision — as discussed by Mary Richardson — I do want to look briefly at the implications of cost-only decisions on anti-poverty and equal opportunities strategies. I do not seek to excuse inefficiencies in managing services, and rigorous attention must be given by local authorities to controllable costs. Analysis of comparative costs reveals that the biggest single difference in the make-up of the costs of care is the percentage devoted to staff wages. Most of those staff are women and in metropolitan areas many will be from black communities. Pay costs could undoubtably be cut by the rationalisation of the workforce, or a dilution of the skill mix, as is more common in private care. The consequence is almost certainly a loss of employment rights and job security which carries over from individuals to communities and local economies. The impact will be disproportionately felt. Responsible use of cost data must include consideration of the impact of changes in policy and operational practice.

Cost data, then, are intrinsically important and are also vital because money is such a powerful lever in policy debates. The PSSRU publications will be invaluable to managers and their staff in costing services as providers or as commissioners. They must assist politicians and the public in using the results responsibly: to balance expanding opportunities for users and their carers with a concern for the economic well-being of communities and their members. To quote Martin Knapp, 'construction and illumination' must continue to be the role of costs research. Let us not return to 'smash and grab'.

The views expressed in this contribution are not necessarily those of Birmingham City Council.